C. Drury Fortnum

Notes on some of the antique and renaissance Gems and

Jewels

In Her Majesty's Collection at Windsor Castle

C. Drury Fortnum

Notes on some of the antique and renaissance Gems and Jewels
In Her Majesty's Collection at Windsor Castle

ISBN/EAN: 9783337135027

Printed in Europe, USA, Canada, Australia, Japan

Cover: Foto ©ninafisch / pixelio.de

More available books at **www.hansebooks.com**

NOTES ON SOME

OF THE

ANTIQUE AND RENAISSANCE

GEMS AND JEWELS

IN HER MAJESTY'S COLLECTION AT WINDSOR CASTLE.

COMMUNICATED TO THE SOCIETY OF ANTIQUARIES

BY

C. DRURY FORTNUM, ESQ., F.S.A.

LONDON:
PRINTED BY NICHOLS AND SONS, 25, PARLIAMENT STREET.

1876.

THE ARCHÆOLOGIA.

Vol. XLV

NOTES ON SOME

OF THE

ANTIQUE AND RENAISSANCE

GEMS AND JEWELS

IN

H.R. MAJESTY'S COLLECTION AT WINDSOR CASTLE.

The collection of antique and other engraved stones, of jewels of the period of the Renaissance, and objects of like class but more recent workmanship, belonging to Her Majesty the Queen, is comparatively little known, although containing several objects of high importance.

On the occasion of a special exhibition of objects of "glyptic art" brought together by the Royal Archæological Institute, and held at the rooms then occupied by that Society in Suffolk Street, Pall Mall, in the month of June 1861, the larger portion of this Royal Collection was graciously contributed, but could only be seen through the glass case which necessarily protected the precious objects it contained.

The series as then shown was examined, as I believe under these disadvantages, by the Rev. C. W. King, M.A. who embodied his observations in a paper published in the eighteenth volume of the Archæological Journal, page 307.

The Royal Collection was also in part exhibited at the South Kensington Museum in 1862, when some of the more remarkable pieces were specially but briefly noted by Mr. J. C. Robinson, in the catalogue of that Loan Collection at page 559, *et seq.*

A more advantageous opportunity of closely examining these valuable objects has been recently afforded to myself, in company with two gentlemen who combine the highest archæological erudition with a profound and accurate technical knowledge of engraved stones and jewels, both of antique and more recent work-

a

manship.   This examination was made with a view to reporting on the collection for Her Majesty's private information.

Availing myself of this privilege to make a preliminary descriptive list of the whole series, I was the more strongly impressed with the great excellence of some of these examples of antique and Renaissance art, and suggested that application might be made for permission to take photographs or drawings of the principal specimens.

That permission has been most liberally accorded, and the accompanying illustrations exhibit some of the more remarkable objects in the Royal Cabinet.

The Collection is, at present, arranged in two glazed tabular cases, that occupy corresponding places on either side of a door of entrance to the elegantly decorated room known as the " Private Audience Chamber " in Windsor Castle. It numbers in all 292 objects of a somewhat heterogeneous character, for among them are works representing the most developed period of the Greco-Roman sculptor's art, others descending through the Byzantine to the period of the Renaissance, and many by the more imitative artists of the seventeenth and eighteenth centuries of our era.   Among the latter not a few are portraits, the majority of which, although not at present recognised, are of considerable interest, and might afford profitable study in tracing, and as far as possible verifying, their likeness to the originals whom they may represent.

My present purpose is not, however, to undertake a work of this nature, but merely to draw attention to, and put more distinctly on record, some of the more important objects of the cabinet, considered from an artistic and archæological point of view ; commencing with those of earlier date.

The autotypes obtained by Her Majesty's gracious permission will greatly enhance the interest of their description, and assist us in appreciating the beauty of the objects which they so accurately portray.

Of those that I have selected as being of more importance than the remainder, the number amounts to 68, viz. antique gems, 16; recent gems and enamelled jewels, 52.   Of these autotypes of 25 have been taken, and wood engravings of two rings and one gem.

Some few antique and modern gems, of minor relative value as to subject or artistic merit, have been included in the following descriptive list, for, although secondary, they are perhaps worthy of being recorded.

.

* Report furnished to Her Majesty, 1872.

No definite history of the formation of this collection can be referred to. The various pieces have been drawn together from time to time, not so much by that peculiar force (shall I borrow a modern term, differently applied, and call it *psychic?*) which gathers objects of a like nature under the directing medium of the amateur, as from an attractive power attaching to royalty, which, acting through numerous family and other connections, induces gifts of portraits, and presents of greater or less artistic and antiquarian merit, in addition to many purchases of objects to which Royal attention has been directed from time to time.

That some of the choicer portraits, as those of Henry VIII. and Elizabeth, have been in the royal cabinet from the period of their production there can be little doubt, notwithstanding any temporary dispersion that may have occurred under the Commonwealth.

They are not, however, mentioned in Van der Doort's catalogue of the objects belonging to Charles I. although he records the large antique cameo and some others.

At the latter end of the last century, when *dilettantism* was in high feather, and works of the antique sculptor's art were sought for and purchased with more avidity than discretion, a premium was offered to the cunning hand that could best imitate the works of classic times; not however without encouraging, to a degree that has never before or since been equalled, those fine artists who, catching much of the antique spirit, produced authentic works of a very high order; the names of Natter, Rega, Pichler, and Pistrucci are representative. Collections of a mixed character were formed accordingly; some from pure love, some from vanity, and some, alas, with a view to dishonest gain. Among these collectors, deceiver or deceived, or both, was Consul Smith, long resident at Venice, who eventually sold the collection he had formed to H.M. George III. The King was further induced to patronise, and in the main pay for, the publication of two folio volumes entitled *Dactyliotheca Smithiana*, Venice, 1767; in which the Consul's cabinet is described by A. F. Gori, and illustrated by 100 well-executed copper-plate engravings. The fact that only three of the specimens that I have deemed worthy of selection and am about to describe, are to be recognised as having formed portions of the Consul's series, will suffice to indicate the inferiority of its contents. The addition of the Smith collection to the other comparatively few but far choicer specimens, and acquisitions since and variously made, have swelled the royal cabinet to its present extent, while, as in like case with the miniatures, drawings, prints, and other rich artistic treasures

a 2

contained in the apartments of Windsor Castle, their systematic gathering together and arrangement in one place is due to the directing energy and judgment of the late Prince Consort.

I will now proceed to describe separately those objects which I have selected as more important, and in doing so have attempted an approximate chronological order, dividing the antique from the Renaissance and modern gems.

Differing in opinion, as I am forced to do on more than one specimen, from our erudite modern authority on antique gems, I feel convinced that such an opportunity as I have had of careful and individual inspection, assisted by minute examination with the lens, would have induced a different *dictum* on his part, had Mr. King enjoyed a similar advantage.

But I am further fortified in advancing my own humble opinion by its agreement with that of Mr. Newton, of Signor Castellani, and, as far as expressed by him in the catalogue of the Loan Collection, with that of Mr. J. C. Robinson.

The measurement is given in inches and lines, one-twelfth of an inch.

CAMEOS AND INTAGLIOS OF ANTIQUE WORKMANSHIP.

193. Intaglio on red or " male " sard; set in a ring, oval. Height 7½ lines. Width 6¼ lines. Cupid bending his bow. Fine Italo-Greek work, probably of about 200 B.C., after the well-known statue.

218. Sunk cameo; *intaglio riliecato*; oval. Height 1 inch 10 lines; width 1 inch 5 lines. (Plate II.)

A Roman male portrait, head in profile, facing to the right of the spectator.

This is a noble work of the best period of Romano-Greek art. The hair, closely cut, is indicated by minutely executed stippling; the brow wrinkled; the ear admirably treated; he is beardless, and bald on the forehead. The general appearance is that of a man between fifty and sixty years of age.

The stone, cracked at the lower end, is backed with glass to strengthen it, and set in a modern gold edging, with loop for suspension.

The art displayed on this gem is of the highest order and the manipulative skill equally excellent; in no place does the *riliero* exceed half a line in depth, while the indications of the muscles of the head and neck are delineated with singular truth and delicacy. This style of antique gem engraving, the " *incavo*

___

The numbers are those now attached to the objects corresponding with the list in the Royal Library.

rilievo" of Mr. King, termed also "Egyptian relief," is but seldom found even in works of smaller size; the present exceptional example is perhaps the finest that has descended to our days. It is by no means improbable that the study of antique gems of this character may have contributed to form the style of sculpture in low relief, on marble and other material, adopted by Donatello and other contemporary Italian sculptors of the fifteenth century. Mr. King does not appear to have noticed this gem in his cursory examination of the Royal Collection, as described by his paper in the Archæological Journal, vol. xviii, p. 309. It did not however escape Mr. Robinson's eye, who refers to it in the catalogue of the Loan Exhibition at South Kensington in 1862 (page 560) as being "perhaps a portrait of one of the Scipios;" in which observation I am inclined to agree. The idea that it may represent Cicero is much more doubtful, neither does it resemble Metellus or Marcellus. The features differ considerably from those of the bust of Cicero, the nose of which is more aquiline and pointed, while the chin is less forward; on that, the treatment of the hair, in short locks, is entirely different; the wart, if it existed, was upon the left cheek and therefore not shown upon the gem. Neither does it correspond with the head of Cicero upon the coins of Magnesia and Lydia, the works of Greek artists.

On the other hand it has considerable affinity to the head of Scipio on the well-known bust in the Capitoline Museum. The closely-cropped hair denotes the warrior, and we learn from Pliny and Gellius that in Scipio's time to shave the beard and hair was fashionable among men of forty and upwards. The scar upon the left forehead could not be shown upon the gem, and it may be objected that, if intended to portray the elder Scipio, so characteristic a mark would not have been neglected by the artist, who might have chosen the other side of his subject; but we know that the head of Scipio (greatly resembling this gem) is similarly placed in the wall-painting representing the marriage of Sophonisba and Massinissa, or rather the surrender of the former to Scipio and her death by poison, found at Pompeii, and which is figured in the Museo Borbonico, vol. i. pl. 34, and in the Iconographie Grecque, pl. 56.

To assume, however, that this fine intaglio (which cannot be favourably rendered by photography) is a contemporary portrait either of Scipio Africanus the elder, or of the younger, might perhaps be too hasty a conclusion; but that it may represent some member of that family is presumable, from the similarity in general character of the features to the only portraits with which we are acquainted.

180. Cameo, on a fine oriental onyx of three strata, clear white, opaque white, and brown. Height 2 inches 5 lines; width 1 inch 11 lines.

Fragment of a head of Jupiter, looking to the right of the spectator. (Plate II.)

A magnificent work of the Augustan age: the beard admirably treated; the wing of the *ægis* is in the brown stratum, the feathers minutely executed. One of the few choice gems from Consul Smith's Collection, and figured in the *Dactyliotheca Smithiana*, pl. I. When perfect this fine cameo must have been 3½ inches high by 2½ wide.

32. Cameo, oblong oval, onyx of two strata, white on brown. Height 7 lines; width 9 lines. Psyche, or more probably a bacchante, lying, with a vase under her right arm and partly covered by an animal's skin; the left arm is raised, the hand behind her head; the hair falling loosely.

Very fine antique work on a beautiful stone. It is set in a ring.

242. Cameo, 7½ inches high by 5¾ wide, of upright oval form, cut upon a rich oriental sardonyx of four or perhaps five strata. (Plate I.)

An imperial male head and bust in profile, facing to the left of the spectator, laurel wreathed and armed with a cuirass fronted by the *ægis*, a sword with eagle-headed hilt at his left side, and the shaft of a spear or sceptre passing over the right shoulder. The rivets with which the cuirass is fastened on either side are concealed by thunderbolts, and the leather straps, issuing from beneath, hang over the arms. Below the *ægis* is a belt or sash, tied round the waist. The grounding is of the dark brown stratum, the head and hair worked in the white, as is also the lance; the wreath in that of honey-brown colour, some of the leaves showing patches of another white stratum. The front of the cuirass is also brown, as are the highly finished feathers which surround the white Gorgon's head: the execution of these is almost equal in careful elaboration to those upon the Jupiter (No. 180); the thunderbolts are white. A raised border cut in the white stratum and capped with brown encircles the portrait, sloping on the inner and enriched with egg-and-dart moulding on the outer side. The portrait conveys the idea of a person more youthful than the original may have been at the period of its execution, the face being well filled out and devoid of lines; its expression sensual, and wanting in mental or physical activity.

The workmanship of this noble cameo is of a very high order, exhibiting a largeness and breadth of style, combined with the highest finish and accuracy in the most minute details. In these qualities it perhaps rivals the well-known Strozzi-Blacas cameo of Augustus now in the British Museum.

That it is a portrait of the Emperor Claudius, and that the execution is contemporary, I have no doubt, notwithstanding that a different judgment has been pronounced and repeated by so learned an authority as the Rev. Mr. King, but under circumstances which probably rendered its close and careful examination by him somewhat difficult.

Compared with the portraits of that emperor in the Vienna and other cameos, &c., figured by Visconti in the *Iconographie Romaine*, vol. ii. pl. 29, and elsewhere, the features would appear to be of an earlier period of life, indeed we can hardly imagine Claudius to have had so youthful an aspect when he had imperial " honours thrust upon him " at the age of 51. But the same allowance must be made for artistic flattery, and we know the effeminate and voluptuous nature of his life and pusillanimous character, which would tend to mollify rather than harden features not otherwise wanting in regularity and beauty. Moreover we may gather from the description by Suetonius,[a] that he was moderately stout, having a thick neck, his complexion and his hair pallid or colourless; but that he was not wanting in some dignity of bearing when standing or seated. These characteristics are admirably rendered in this cameo.

Mr. King in the *Archæological Journal*, vol. xviii. p. 312, states it to be " an easily recognised portrait of Constantius II."[b] He notices that the *ægis* is covered with eagle's feathers in lieu of scales, and the delicate execution of the Gorgon's head; but he writes, " the face is without much character, and may belong to any of the sons of Constantine; " and, " here, as in all works of the far-advanced decline, the artist has expended his chief pains upon the accessories," &c.

In venturing to differ from so erudite a writer on antique gems, I would suggest that some of his remarks would seem to be contradictory in themselves; no such important work of the " lower imperial period," with which I am acquainted, exhibits, as this does, that large character and breadth of treatment combined with so careful a finish and highly artistic management of the hair and other details, among which the Medusa's head is, as Mr. King writes, " in itself a perfect gem for delicate execution." If so, it can hardly be " of the far advanced decline," such as the well-known and comparatively barbarous works of the period of the sons of Constantine, nor this grand cameo " an easily recognised portrait of Constantius II." Mr. Robinson, on the other hand, remarks, " The admirable style of art displayed in the noble cameo renders it one of the most important works of the kind now extant;" an opinion in which I fully agree.

Being therefore accepted upon its own evidence as without doubt a work of the first century, we need not look for the original among Constantine's sons, but rather to the members of the family of Augustus, whose features it, in a weak degree, recalls. A glance over their portraits fixes attention only to that of the grand nephew to Augustus, Tiberius Claudius Nero, the son of the elder Drusus by Antonia, and brother of Germanicus.

Compared with the heads upon the coins of Claudius, there is a similarity, but with some difference, the nose being more aquiline upon the gem; but we must bear in mind that upon the coins of that period the heads were more or less idealized, and modelled after a Greek type of the features of Augustus, a habit which prevailed to a greater or less extent even to the time of Vitellius. The cameo, however, greatly resembles the laureated head upon the medal figured by Mongez in the *Iconog. Rom.* pl. xxvii. No. 5, around which is the legend TI*berius* CLAVDIVS CAESAR AV*Gustus Pontifex Maximus* TRibunitia *Potestate* IM*Perator*.

The bronze bust in the Louvre, figured on the same plate in that work, differs from the cameo in the more pointed extremity of the nose; the unfortunate fracture of the latter has slightly chipped that feature, enough perhaps to have rendered this difference more apparent. The bust is that of an older man. The cameo occupies an intermediate place in point of resemblance between this bronze and the colossal head of the deified Claudius in Spain, and figured in the same plate; both differ from and both resemble it. The statue in the Lateran is also of his more advanced period in life, but not without considerable resemblance to the head upon the cameo. There is also a bust of Claudius in the British Museum.

We next turn to the cameos which are figured on plate 29 of the work of Mongez. The first of these is believed to represent Claudius and Messalina, with their two children Octavia and Britannicus, drawn in a triumphal car by two centaurs, and believed by the Chevalier Mongez to figure the triumph of Claudius over the Britons. It is a work of inferior merit, perhaps of local origin, but ascribed to a period shortly after the event represented. In this the features of Claudius more nearly approach in character to those of Augustus. We can gather but little from the portion of a second cameo figured on the same plate, the heads being all in full face; but on the third there delineated, the well-known gem in the Imperial Cabinet at Vienna, we have on its right side the profile bust of Claudius (about which most antiquaries are agreed) accompanied by Messalina or Agrippina, and facing those of two younger persons, variously described as Britannicus and Octavia, or Germanicus and the elder Agrippina, and by Eckhel as the elder

Drusus and Antonia. In this cameo the head of Claudius faces to the right of the spectator, and is crowned with a chaplet of oak; the features are less plump; lines upon the cheek and around the mouth denote a more advanced age than on the Queen's gem. The general character of the face is however very similar, and the style of the hair round the back of the neck, &c. quite agrees.

Other gems of less importance, believed to represent Claudius, exist in cabinets. Three are in the Marlborough (Arundel) Collection. Perhaps the most important of these is that numbered 122; on a fine sardonyx the bust of Claudius, oak-wreathed and wearing the *ægis*, looking to the left of the spectator. This portrait bears a strong affinity to that on the Queen's gem, but represents the Emperor at a later period of his life, in this respect approaching more nearly to the cameo at Vienna. A photograph of it may be seen on pl. xiv. of Mr. Soden Smith's catalogue of the Loan Exhibition of Jewellery in 1872 at the South Kensington Museum.

Bearing more or less a general resemblance to each of these various portraits, we can come to no other conclusion than that this grand cameo must represent Claudius, either at the period when, associated with Caligula in the consulate (A.U. 793), he was nominated to the office of *sacerdos*, and may be here portrayed in the assumed quality of the Latin Jupiter; or shortly after the time when, thrust trembling into power by the pretorians, he became Emperor in the forty-first year of our era.

This cameo came into the Royal Collection in the time of King Charles I, but whence we know not. It is entered in Van der Doort's catalogue of that unfortunate monarch's collection as, "Imprimis, a large oval cracked and mended agate stone of four colours, one on the top of another, first brown and then white and brown again and then white; wherein is cut an emperor's head in a laurel, side-faced; kept in a leather case; which agate the King had when he was prince."

There is a note on the margin which further states, "This was cracked and broken in former time by the Lady Somerset, when her husband was Lord Chamberlain." * Except for the effects of this unhappy accident, by which it was broken into eleven pieces, the work is in a perfectly genuine and original condition. A small piece is wanting from behind the neck, as are also the bows of the ribbon which secures the laurel chaplet, and some other less important fragments, together with a portion of the surrounding raised edge. It is now cemented together and framed in a gilt metal cording and edge.

* Robert Earl of Somerset was Lord Chamberlain from 1613 to 1615.

279. Intaglio on a circular and convex oriental onyx of brown and white strata. Total diameter 11 lines. One of the Dioscuri; the star on the head, a spear in the left hand, the horse at his side. Good antique work, in the original gold mounting as a circular pendant, with loop for suspension to a neck-chain; it is backed with gold, and has a beaded edging.

This is another interesting instance of the use to which some of the larger antique intaglios were applied by the Roman jewellers.

30. Cameo; oval; onyx of four strata, red, white, red, and white. Height 7 lines; width 5½ lines. A warrior kneeling, with lance over the right shoulder; the Gorgon on his shield; probably antique work of the latter end of the third century.

16. Cameo; upright oval; sardonyx of three strata, dark brown, greyish white, and rich brown; a fine stone. Height 17½ lines; width 11½ lines. Female portrait in low relief to the left; probably antique Roman work of the third century, and perhaps the portrait of a queen.

It is mounted in enamelled gold-work of the sixteenth or early seventeenth century; a white corded framing with ring above for suspension and another below for a pendant drop, attached to the framing by shoulder-plates enamelled with colour.

This mounting is precisely similar to to that on No. 131 of this list, and on two cameos in the Marlborough Collection, Nos. 571-8. (Maskelyne Cat.)

24. Cameo; circular; onyx of two strata, white and brown. Diameter 14 lines. (Plate III.)

A naked female seated, towards whom a small figure of a faun or satyr approaches holding a wreath in the left hand, surrounded by a raised border reserved in the stone, probably antique Roman work of the third century A.D. The setting may be English and of the seventeenth century. It consists of a gold border of embossed work enamelled with flowers; the back is decorated with double hearts surrounded by a wreath of laurel, and an unintelligible inscription: the whole forming a pretty ornament.

224. Cameo; oval; onyx of two strata, white on grey. Height 7 lines; width 9 lines.

A man and a boy gathering fruit (grapes?). Mr. King, referring to this gem, considers that the subject represents Bacchus and Ampelus. (Plate II.) Late Roman work in enamelled setting of the seventeenth century, with vine-leaves at the back.

2. Cameo; upright; oval onyx of three strata, dark brown, opaque white, and honey brown. Height 1 inch; width 7½ lines. Head of Isis looking to the

left of the spectator. Of antique Roman art, but somewhat coarse in the execution.

15. Cameo; upright oval; sardonyx of two strata set in a ring. Height 10 lines; width 7 lines. Female bust to the left, holding ears of corn on a branch. Antique Roman, of good style, but rather coarsely executed.

234. Cameo; oval; sardonyx of two strata, white on brown. Height 10½ lines; width 7½ lines. Portrait head, to the left, laureated; perhaps of Commodus. Coarse late Roman work, not improbably colonial, in enamelled setting of the seventeenth century.

250. Cameo; oval; on *onice zaffarina* of two strata, white on blue. Height 7½ lines; width 10 lines. A lion couchant to the right. A work of the later Roman period set in a ring. Mr. King refers to this gem as antique.

240. Cameo; onyx of three strata, red, white, and red. Length 9 lines; height 6½ lines. A man in a *biga* driving to the right of the spectator.

A very spirited work, which, although not without a suspicion of Odelli, may be of the later Roman Imperial period.

34. Cameo; oblong oval; on a fine sardonyx of three strata, black, blue, and brown. Height 17 lines; width 2 inches. (Plate II.)

Two helmeted male heads facing each other, inclosed in a raised rim or border reserved in the blue stratum, in which the heads also are worked, the helmets being in the brown. The cutting is in low relief, probably colonial, of the third or may be early in the fourth century, on a magnificent *sardonica oniciata*. I agree with Mr. King in thinking it to be a work of the decadence; but whether portraits of some of the sons of Constantine is less certain. That on the left would seem to be the elder; on the helmet of the other a lion is represented in relief. At the back an *anubis-abraxas* is engraved in intaglio, surrounded by a Gnostic inscription; probably work of a later period, and very coarsely executed.

BYZANTINE, RENAISSANCE, AND MODERN WORKS.

43. Large pendent ornament *(piccio petto)* of enamelled gold, of the latter half of the sixteenth century. It is set with cameos of various periods, and is probably of Venetian workmanship. (Plate II.)

In the centre is an oblong square cameo, on onyx of two strata, white and grey in very high relief. Height 13 lines; width 20 lines.

The subject is Joseph receiving his brethren on their second visit to Egypt. It is a composition of many figures. Joseph is seated on a sort of throne; to the right before him, one kneels, holding the cup which had been found in his sack. Of the remainder, four stand surrounding; one holds the sack; the others are merely indicated by their heads seen behind the group.

The figures are cut in the white stratum of the stone, leaving the ground of a grey colour. The artistic workmanship is of a very peculiar character, having an antique sentiment, but of the late decline. It is much undercut, and is probably Byzantine of the sixth or seventh century, and, if so, a most rare and interesting example of the sculptor's art of that period.

Surrounding the central and more important stone, the enamelled gold framing is further enriched with several smaller cameos in *pietra dura*, for the most part of Venetian workmanship and of the period of the ornament. They represent negroes' heads, in some cases relieved on the white ground; three are arranged above the centre, and are surmounted by one immediately beneath the ring for suspension. Three other cameos are similarly placed on the lower side; of these the central one is of oblong oval form and probably antique workmanship, representing a Pan regarding a recumbent Venus, cut in the black stratum, whom a Cupid reveals; it is of good art, and on an onyx of three strata: on the left of this (as seen by the spectator) is a helmeted male head to the left, and on the right an imperial head to the right, while another negro is suspended from beneath. On the left side of the central piece another cameo is set, a negro—black on grey—from which again another is suspended as a drop; and on the right, to correspond, is an imperial head to the left, which may be an antique retouched, and from which another drop is hanging, set with a negro's head, as on the other side. The back is enamelled in the centre with foliated sprays in black upon the gold, while on either side a dragon is emerging from a cornucopia; strap-work and other ornaments cover the remainder of the framing.

This noble jewel, remarkable in itself from its unusual size, being $5\frac{1}{4}$ inches long by $3\frac{1}{2}$ inches wide, is still more so from the rare cameo which forms its central enrichment.

210. Cameo; oriental onyx of two strata, black and white; St. George and the Dragon, riding to the right, with his name in Greek letters. Height $9\frac{1}{2}$ lines; width $7\frac{1}{4}$ lines. (Plate II.)

Byzantine work of the tenth or eleventh century.

211. Cameo; on a ruby of pale colour and clear lustre. About 8 lines high by 6 lines wide. Portrait of Louis XII of France, crowned, head to the right.

This is a remarkable and rare work of the latter end of the fifteenth or early part of the sixteenth century. Mr. King considers it may be the earliest known Renaissance portrait in cameo on so hard a stone, and with considerable probability ascribes it to Domenico dei Camei, who executed the portrait of Ludovico il Moro on the same material.

CAMEO, FULL SIZE
Profile of a Queen.

It is mounted in a modern setting of gold as a ring, enamelled with *fleurs-de-lis* on the shoulders; on the gold plate at the back of the bezel is engraven the inscription "*Loys XII⁰ Roy de France décédé 1 Janvier, 1515.*"

The gold casing or rim, with claws holding the stone, is old, and it would seem that a more ancient mounting, made however subsequently to a chip on the edge of the stone, had been injured or altered and in part grafted upon an enamelled setting, that is manifestly of modern workmanship and in very bad taste.

16. A fine Italian pendent ornament (*piccia petto*) of the best artistic period of the sixteenth century, and probably of Florentine workmanship. (Plate III.)

It consists of an enamelled gold framing to a central oval medallion. The original of this has been replaced by a male head in cameo, looking to the right of the beholder, on an onyx of two strata, clear and opaque brown; it is of more recent workmanship, the setting of which appears to be of the latter end of the eighteenth century or even later.

This cameo, in the mock classic style, without head covering, but with drapery fastened on the shoulder, bears no sort of resemblance to the well-known portrait of Francis I. as has been suggested.

The three pendent gems beneath are also, unfortunately, additions of the same period to replace others. That in the middle is a modern cameo of the Blessed Virgin, on turquoise, on each side of which is an inferior one of the eighteenth century, set round respectively with rubies and emeralds, and which have been the bezels or tables cut from finger-rings of that period.

It is desirable that these unsightly hangers should be removed, retaining perhaps, the central medallion, as also the pendent pearls.

On the enamelled gold framing, at the sides, are figures of Cupid and Mars; another cupid or *amorino* is flying above the central medallion, and beneath is a sea-monster. Pendent pearls, table diamonds, and rubies enrich other parts, while at the back, occupying the whole of the centre, are enamelled figures in bold relief of Apollo and Daphne, having a *cartouche* inscribed DAPHNEM . PHEBVS . AMAT; on other labels are names of the figures on the front, CVPID . VERVS . &c.

In respect to workmanship this is one of the finest ornamental jewels of the best period of the *cinque-cento* (unfortunately not intact), and is an admirable example of the goldsmith's and enameller's skill and of artistic design at that period.

Mr. King refers to this pendant in his paper in the *Archæological Journal* (vol. xviii. p. 309),* and singularly enough concluded that the central cameo and those hanging from beneath are of the same period as the ornament itself. He considers the first to be "an excellent profile head of Francis I." of France, and strangely confirms that idea by describing the sea-monster beneath as a "salamander." He overlooked the fact that this cameo is in a recent "casing" or mounting, and is an addition of the last century, or even of more modern time, and that the creature is an imaginary marine and not an igneous monster. He also speaks of the pendent cameos beneath as "works of the same age" (as the ornament), "the best a veiled head of Ceres on a large and fine turquoise."

These errors in Mr. King's judgment could only have arisen from the disadvantageous circumstances under which he must have examined the jewel.

Its total length is about 4¼ inches, width about 2¼ inches.

74. A "George." The group of St. George and the Dragon riding to the right is in *ronde bosse*, and formed of finely chased and enamelled gold in a circular surrounding; the figure of the princess is seen kneeling in the background. On the back is green enamel. Diameter 1¼ inch. (Plate III.)

Probably German work of the early half of the sixteenth century.

It is now inclosed under glass in a gilt and enamelled box framing of the period of George IV., which is made to open, and is surrounded by the garter and motto in blue enamel.

131. Double cameo, on an oriental onyx of three strata, dark brown, blue, and rich golden brown; oval. Height of stone 2 inches. Width 1¼ inch. On the dark stratum a negro's head, three-quarter face, looking to the right of the spectator. It is worked in a sort of *intaglio rilevato*, a surrounding rim being left of the same depth as the most prominent part of the head. The flesh is without, but the eyes are strongly marked by having a high polish. He wears a cuirass, and ear-rings are in the ears.

On the other side is a female bust in profile, also looking to the right, carved in the blue layer on the darker ground; she wears a wreath of vine-leaves, which, together with the more prominent portion of the dress, is executed in the rich honey-brown stratum of the stone. There is something in the execution of this head that gives rise to the suspicion that it may have been an antique, injured and again worked over. It is mounted as a pendant in white enamelled and gold framing with loop attachments picked out in red, that above having a ring for

* See also "Antique Gems and Rings," 2d ed. 1872, p. 323.

suspension, the lower one probably for a hanging pearl, which has been removed. This mounting is precisely similar to that of No. 16 of this collection, and to that of Nos. 578 (Arundel) and 571 (Besborough) in the Marlborough Cabinet (Maskelyne Cat.), and in all probability of about the same period as the negro cameo which it surrounds. The gem is of admirable execution, and might with reasonable probability be ascribed to the same period, and perhaps to the same artist, as the fine portrait of Elizabeth.

73. Pendant, in enamelled gold; setting a *baroque* or monster pearl, which forms the body of a mermaid. She holds a mirror in the left hand and is dressing her hair with a comb held in the right. The tail is set with rubies on green enamel.

The figure is suspended by two chains to an ornamental flower with ring above. A mother-o'-pearl mask hanging over the figure and three pendent pearls below having diamond shoulders are modern additions. The former ought to be removed. (Plate III.)

This is a fine Italian jewel of the sixteenth century.

158. Ring of enamelled gold set with a cameo on garnet, a mask or bacchic head of fine contemporary work.

The enamelling and goldsmith's work are also of great excellence. A hole at the base of the hoop, with internal screw-worm, was probably fitted with a squirt by which liquids could be projected through another hole in the mouth of the mask. This might have been a toy used by bluff King Hal in his merry mood.

91. Cameo; oriental onyx of brown on a clear stratum. Height 10 lines; width 8 lines. Head of the Saviour in full face.

A "Veronica" or "Volto Santo." Fine work of the sixteenth century.

91. Cameo; large oblong oval agate of three strata, brown, opaque white, and clear brown. Height 1 inch 4 lines; width 2½ inches. The Adoration of the Magi. (Plate III.)

A minutely executed work of high finish, of the earlier half or middle of the sixteenth century, perhaps the work of Matteo del Nazzaro; or possibly of Dominicus Romanus, who executed the cameo in the Florentine collection, representing the entrance into Siena of Cosimo I. The elaboration of the figures, which are deeply undercut, and the adaptation to the strata of the stone, are worthy of note.

265. Cameo; on a fine, nearly circular, sardonyx of three strata, dark brown, white, and golden brown. Height 1 inch 5½ lines; width 1 inch 1½ lines. (Plate IV.)

A portrait of Henry VIII. in cap and feather, within a raised border; three-quarter face, looking to the right of the spectator. He wears a slashed doublet. It is in the original simple gold setting as a pendant, and was probably cut by the same hand as No. 285.

285. Cameo; long oval. Height 2¼ inches; width 3 inches 1 line. (Plate IV.) On a splendid oriental sardonyx of three strata, dark brown, bluish white, and clear honey brown. Portraits of Henry VIII. and of his child Edward VI.; the former three-quarter face, looking to the right of the spectator and towards the young Edward, on whose left shoulder his right hand is placed; the latter, in full face, wears a baby's cap, holding a flower in his right hand. Henry is richly dressed in slashed doublet, cap, and feather; these, except the feather, which is in the white, are worked in the honey-brown stratum, as also the beard, the child's hair, and a ring upon Henry's first finger. The faces and hands are in the white, as also the slashes of the doublet. The grounding is on the dark stratum, and a raised surrounding border is reserved in the stone capped with the upper brown layer.

On the reverse is an unfinished intaglio following the outlines of the cameo, except that the child's cap is similar in form to that of the father, but without feather, and the boy's head looks older.

Mr. King suggests that the intaglio at the back may have been cut in order to give light through the stone, but it does not render the stone translucent, and it is remarkable that the child's cap should differ in form from that in the cameo. He refers to a similar example in the portrait of Edward VI., which is one among the Devonshire gems (in the necklace, No. 18), and suggests that these and other similar works may have been executed from portraits by Holbein, &c., sent to Italy, and there worked in cameo by "the Vincentino, or Nazaro, then in the height of his reputation" (Archæological Journal, xviii. p. 309).

There can be no doubt that it is by the same artist as No. 265.

251. Cameo; onyx of dark brown and blue-white strata; a portrait on nicolo of a man, three-quarter face, wearing a high conical hat with feather in front, turn-down collar, and a circular pendent jewel or medal. Height 8 lines; width 7 lines. (Plate IV.)

The execution of this portrait (which may be intended for Sydney or Essex), although differing from the singularly low-relief of those of Henry VIII., has much about it that would lead to the supposition that it may be a later work by the same hand.

255. Cameo, on a fine oval oriental sardonyx of three strata, dark brown, white, and brown. Height 1½ inch; width 1 inch 2½ lines. (Plate IV.)

Portrait bust of Queen Elizabeth looking to the left of the spectator, surrounded by a raised border; the hair and part of the dress in the upper brown layer, the flesh in the white. It is mounted in a thin enamelled gold edging.

A fine work of the time of Elizabeth, and probably by the same hand as Nos. 263 and 284.

284. Cameo on oriental onyx of two strata, oval. Height 1 inch 7 lines; width 1 inch 5 lines. (Plate IV.)

Portrait of Queen Elizabeth(?), also looking to the left, in a raised border; the dress is diapered. An unfinished work.

The outline of the features and the expression of this head differ considerably from those of the other portrait cameos of Elizabeth, as far as one can judge from so unfinished a work. The question has indeed arisen as to whether this may not have been commenced as a portrait of Mary, and perhaps left incomplete by the artist, who, from circumstances political or religious, may have absented himself from the country, or lost court patronage. His work is lost sight of during that Queen's reign, to be again resumed under Elizabeth.

263. Cameo; oval, on a superb oriental sardonyx of three strata, dark brown, grey, and honey brown. Height 2 inches 7½ lines; width 2 inches. (Plate IV.)

Bust portrait of Queen Elizabeth looking to the left of the beholder, within a raised border.

The ground is of the dark layer; the flesh, portion of the head-dress, the frill, and boddice, in the white; the hair, edge of the frill, ornaments, puffed sleeves, and stomacher, in the upper brown. It is mounted in a simple gold edging with claws.

This admirable work is in a large style, combined with most minute execution of the details, and is probably by the same hand as the two preceding cameos.

Unfortunately we are left without any positive information as to the name and country of this excellent artist, no signed specimen or sufficiently definite historical record being known to us.

A comparison of all the cameos represented on Plate IV. leads, as I think, to the following inference: First, that the portraits of Philip and Magarita are certainly not by the same hand as those of Henry or Elizabeth; if therefore the former (as is not improbable) are the work of Jacopo da Trezzo, the latter are certainly not by him.

There is considerable difference in the treatment of the portraits of Henry VIII.

c

and those of Elizabeth, enough to give rise to the suspicion of another hand, may be master and pupil—if so, the latter the more able ; or the difference may, as I suspect, only arise from a modification and improvement in manner consequent upon longer practice of his art. We must, moreover, bear in mind that the earlier works are nearly in full face, those of Elizabeth in profile, which would permit of a more ready exhibition of a higher relief.

Walpole's idea that Valerio Belli (Vicentino) was their author is refuted by the difference of his manner, and the fact that he died in 1546, twelve years before Elizabeth's accession. The same reasons apply to Giovanni del Castel Bolognese. Mr. King suggests that the Henry VIII. may be by Luca Penni. Why not, with equal probability, Jacobus Thromus, who, Gori tells us, cut the arms of Mary of England upon a diamond about 1557? (Hist. Dact. p. 180.)

But Coldoré is supposed to have a stronger claim, although I fear he lived too late to have executed the portraits of Henry and Edward, assuming them to be contemporary. The latter was born in 1537, and is represented upon our cameo at somewhat under three years old ; Coldoré's head of Henry IV. on ruby is dated 1590, half a century later; the sapphire in the Lotureq Collection (recently dispersed by public sale at Messrs. Sotheby's), engraved by him with portraits of Henry IV. and Marie di Médicis, face to face, is signed " Coldoré," and dated " 1605 ; " and Mariette tells us that he worked for Louis XIII., who did not reign till 1610. Assuming, therefore, that Coldoré cut the gem of Henry and Edward when twenty years of age, he would have been ninety when Louis XIII. came to the throne of France.

It is believed that he was invited to England by Elizabeth, and Mariette ascribes to him, without doubt, the portrait of that Queen in the Orleans Collection. It is moreover possible that the portraits of Henry and his children may have been executed from designs taken at an earlier period, and that this, and the fact of his being a younger artist, may account for their differing in manner from those of Elizabeth, which he could have modelled from the life at a later date. We may however, as I believe, look nearer home for the engraver of the portraits of Henry VIII. and of Edward. At page 108 of the first volume of Mr. Wornum's edition of "Walpole's Anecdotes of Painting in England" (Lond. 1849), we read : " John Mustyan, born at Enguien, is recorded as Henry's arras-maker ; John de Mayne as his seal graver; and *Richard Astyll as his graver of stones;*" while a note at the foot of the page tells us that " Hillyard (the same person, probably, of whom more hereafter) cut the images of Henry VIII. and his children on a sardonyx, in the collection of the Duke of Devonshire. The

Earl of Exeter has such another. Lady Mary Wortley had the head of the same
king on a little stone in a ring; cameo on one side, and intaglio on the other."
A second note to Atsyll states, " with a fee of 20*l.* a-year."

There must however be some confusion here, for Nicholas Hilliard, the limner,
the person "probably" referred to, was not born until the year 1547, in which
year Henry VIII. died. Nor have we any record of engraved stones or cameos
worked by that able miniature painter and goldsmith. I suspect therefore that
this statement of Walpole's must have been in error, and that the real author of
these portraits of Henry and of Edward was no other than Richard Atsyll, the
King's graver of stones. Walpole's inaccuracy is further shown when writing
of Valerio Vicentino, at pages 188-9 of the same volume, to whose hand he
ascribes some of the portraits in cameo of Elizabeth; and where he states that
"The Duke of Devonshire has several of his works, two profiles in cameo of
Queen Elizabeth, another gem with the head of Edward VI., cameo on one side
and intaglio on the other," a characteristic which at once points to the same
artist as he who cut the Henry and Edward in Her Majesty's collection. I have
already shown that *il Vicentino* could not have engraved the cameos of Elizabeth,
having died twelve years before that Queen's accession.

Of Atsyll we hear further that he was continued in the royal service under
Edward VI., for, among the accounts of the Royal Household in the Trevelyan
Papers, published by the Camden Society in 1857, in vol. i. p. 195, we read,
" Item to Richard Atzell, graver of stones, C^s" or five pounds, a quarter's salary;
and similar payments are entered in December of the second year of Edward VI.,
and in March and Midsummer of the third year of Edward VI. (Vol. ii.
pp. 18, 25, 31.)

From this time to the accession of Elizabeth a period of only eight years passes,
but during which I have been unable to find any further note of Atsyll or Atzell,
nor am I aware of any royal portraits attributable to the same hand.* It is not
unreasonable to suppose that during this interval, if still living, he may willingly
or otherwise have retired from office under the Crown, and developed his artistic
style into that shown in such perfection on the larger portrait of Elizabeth in
the Royal Collection. May he not have taken refuge abroad from the persecu-
tions and troubles of Mary's reign, improving his art under the guidance of some
Italian or French engraver ?

All these cameos represent Elizabeth when young and within a few years after

* His name is not referred to among the new year's gifts offered to Philip and Mary in 1556.

her accession. Some fifteen or more are known; but an interesting entry, which would account for their being so numerous, is to be found in Nichols's Progresses of Elizabeth (i. 282), where, accompanying the description of her visit to Hunsdon House in 1571, is an engraving, copied from Vertue, showing the Queen in procession surrounded by her Knights of the Garter. Conspicuous among these, according to Vertue, are Dudley Earl of Leicester, Lord Hunsdon, Lord Burghley, Charles Howard, Admiral (afterwards Lord) Nottingham, Lord Clinton, Lord Russell, and Lord Sussex—seven in all then present—"each of them having a ribband about his neck with a small gem or intaglio¹ appended to it; thereon a profile of her Majesty's countenance; which additional ornament, it is conjectured, was designed to represent these noblemen to be the Queen's favourites." It is probably one of such that is noticeable on the cameo portrait No. 251.

In an interesting paper by Mr. George Scharf, F.S.A., published in the Archæological Journal, vol. xxiii. p. 131, it is shown that the painting referred to as representing Queen Elizabeth's visit to Hunsdon House in 1571, according to the statement of Vertue, is wrongly so described; the occasion depicted being her Majesty's procession to Blackfriars, to celebrate the marriage of Anne daughter of John Lord Russell with Lord Herbert, son of the Earl of Worcester, on the 16th June, 1600. And further, that six of the noblemen represented as being Knights of the Garter, and who are also decorated with a medallion of the Queen, are Edward fourth Earl of Worcester, father of the bridegroom; the Lord High Admiral, Charles Earl of Nottingham; George Carey, second Lord Hunsdon, Lord Chamberlain; Henry Brooke, sixth Lord Cobham, Warden of the Cinque Ports; George Clifford, Earl of Cumberland; and Thomas, first Lord Howard of Walden, afterwards Earl of Suffolk, Constable of the Tower; and not those named by Vertue, as above. The seventh Garter is not noticed by Mr. Scharf; he is seen in the picture behind, and between Nottingham and Cobham. I have not however been able to discover any entries of payments made to any "graver of stones," neither to Atsill nor Coldoré, nor to her jewellers, John Spilman nor Peter Trender, for any of these portrait gems, nor are they recorded among presents made by her Majesty.

Among gifts offered to her Majesty, may be noted in 1581, "By eight maskers in Christmas weeke;" "A flower of golde garnished with sparcks of diamonds, rubyes, and ophales, with an agate of her Majestis phisnamy, and a perle pendante, with devices painted in it."² And in the list of the Queen's wardrobe in

¹ I suspect this word has been somewhat inaccurately applied.

² Nichols's Progresses, vol. ii. p. 389.

1600 we find, among objects received by Sir Thos. Gorges, Knight, of Mrs. Mary Radcliffe, " Item, one jewele of golde like a dasye, and small flowers aboute it garnished with sparks of diamondes and rubies, with her Majesties picture graven within a garnet, and a sprigge of three branches, garnished with sparks of rubies, one perle in the topp, and a small pendaunte of sparks of diamondes."

This fine series of royal cameos in Her Majesty's cabinet is unrivalled, the four gems of like character in the Devonshire *parure* being relatively of minor importance: two of these portray Elizabeth, another the young Edward, already referred to, and the fourth a group of Henry VIII., with Mary, Edward, and Elizabeth. A similar quadruple cameo is, as I learn, in the possession of Captain Peel. The Hawkins collection contains one of Elizabeth; one belonged to Mr. Webb. The fine cameo of Elizabeth (ascribed by Gori to Coldoré) of the Orleans collection is now in the Hermitage at St. Petersburg, where, as I am informed, are also some other cameo portraits of that Queen. One is in the Royal Collection at the Hague; this, like all the rest, in showing the left side of the face, has the hair and head-dress, as also the ruff, in very high relief; and another, a three-quarter length figure, is in the South Kensington Museum. I am disposed to regard these two last as of later date than those in the Royal and Devonshire collections.

Three are in the Bibliothèque at Paris, thus described by Chabouillet: " No. 371. Elizabeth reine d'Angleterre. Buste. Sardonyx à 3 couches. H. 55 mill. L. 40 mill. Monture en or. Nous attribuons ce beau camée à Julien de Fontenay, dit Coldoré, graveur sur pierres fines et valet de chambre de Henri IV." He then repeats, and accepts as probable, Mariette's tradition, that Coldoré had been invited to England to take the Queen's portrait in cameo, he being then unrivalled in that art. " No. 372. Elizabeth reine d'Angleterre. Buste. Sardonyx 3 couches; monture en or émaille, ornée de rubis;" and " No. 373. Elizabeth reine d'Angleterre. Buste. Sardonyx à 3 couches."

Two are at Vienna, described by Arneth, p. 102, taf. ii. 22, and taf. v. One of these, which I well recollect as a magnificent work, he considers finer than that in the Bibliothèque at Paris, or the Orleans gem.

He also repeats the story that Coldoré was sent to England by Henri IV. to

Nichols's Progresses, vol. iii. p. 512.   Vol. ii. pl. 74, p. 159.
For a cast of this gem, and for other valuable information, I am indebted to our Director, Mr. A. W. Franks, F.R.S.   Cat. des Camées, &c. de la Bib. Imp. Paris.
Arneth, Joseph von, die Cinque Cento Cameen, &c. im K. K. Munz und Antiken Cabinette zu Wien.

take the Queen's portrait. The final ring given by Elizabeth to Essex, now belonging to Lord John Thynne, is set with a cameo of that Queen, not on onyx, but cut upon a garnet. Another portrait in cameo on turquoise is set in a pendant belonging to Miss Elizabeth Wild, in whose family it has been preserved since its gift by Elizabeth, as a christening present to its first owner.

Another portrait cameo of Queen Elizabeth, on an onyx of opaque white and brownish yellow, of similar general character, but rather coarse workmanship, was recently sold at Messrs. Christie and Manson's. It was mounted as a pendant in enamelled gold set with stones and of modern French workmanship. (May, 1874.)

265. Cameo on white and clear grey agate. Height 9 lines; width 7½ inches. (Plate IV.)

Portrait bust of Philip II., looking to the left. A fine work of his time, perhaps by the same hand as No. 266, but not so highly elaborated.

266. Cameo; oval; oriental onyx of three layers; clear, opaque white, and brown. Height 1 inch 8½ lines; width 1¼ inch. (Plate IV.)

Bust of Philip II. looking to the left of the spectator, in armour and with a mantle, which, falling from the shoulder, is worked in the brown stratum. The head is bare, the flesh in the white stratum, and polished. Van der Doort, in his catalogue, describes what is in all likelihood the same stone as having been given to Charles I. in 1637.[*]

This is clearly by another hand than that which worked the portraits of Henry VIII. or of Elizabeth. Mr. King ascribes it, and not without probability, to Jacopo da Trezzo, and as by the same as "the more important one, No. 200 Besborough gems." He also refers another cameo on yellow crystal (No. 366 Arundel) to that artist, a portrait of Philip, or of his son Don Carlos. In the South Kensington Museum is a fine cameo of Philip II. seemingly by the same hand. Another is in the Imperial Cabinet at Vienna;[*] and another in the Bibliothèque at Paris. There are three in the Florentine Collection.

287. Cameo; oval; white on grey onyx. Height 1 inch 5 lines; width 1 inch 1 line. (Plate IV.)

---

[*] " Item: Another agate stone of King Philip of Spain, the head being white, the breast brownish, and the ground transparent like to a glass; delivered to me by the King." " Given to the King, 1637."

Anoth. die Cinque Cento Cameen, &c. taf. 1, 82. p. 60.

Chabouillet. Cat. p. 74. No. 370. Philippe II. Roi d'Espagne. Buste. Onyx a 2 couches. H. 36 mill.; L. 25.

Female portrait looking to the left of the beholder; a highly elaborated and beautiful work of the sixteenth century, ascribed by Gori to Giovanni Bernardi, "Jo: del Castro Bononiensis," and to be the portrait of Margarita of Austria, daughter of the Emperor Charles V., the wife of Ottavio Farnese, Duke of Parma and Governor of the Netherlands. She is young and beautiful; her hair in plaited bands crossing each other and intertwined with strings of pearls. She wears a dress with a high collar, turned back, and puffed sleeves; a frill is about her neck, and a double row of pearls over her dress, which is richly braided. This cameo is engraved in the *Dactyliotheca Smithiana*, under No. C., and may probably be the stone referred to by Vasari, in his notice of Giovanni di Castel Bolognese, stating that he executed this work in competition with Valerio Vicentino.

58. Cameo; oval; onyx of three strata, grey and brown. Height 1½ inch; width 11 lines. Bust of Pallas to the right.

Good work of the sixteenth century; in enamelled setting of the seventeenth or eighteenth century.

236. Cameo; onyx of two strata, clear grey and white. Height 1 inch 3½ lines; width 1 inch. Two portraits (?), that of a man on the white stratum, and of a negress on the grey.

Good work of the sixteenth or seventeenth century, probably Venetian.

47. Cameo; oval; white opaque agate on a clear stratum. Height 7 lines; width 9½ lines. Cupid, Amphitrite, and a dolphin.

Fine work of the later years of the sixteenth century.

41. Cameo; oval; portrait; female bust, to the right; the head in carnelian with drapery of amethyst. Total height 1 inch 11½ lines; width 1 inch 5½ lines. The crown jewelled and with black enamelling; the framing of gold, with black enamel; at the back strap-work ornamentation in coloured translucent enamel; sixteenth century.

45. Cameo; oval; onyx of two strata, white and grey. Height 10 lines; width 8 lines. The full face of a bacchic boy.

Fine work of the sixteenth century.

36. Cameo; agate of three strata, red, yellow, and brown. Height 14 lines; width 11 lines. The Virgin and Child, with St. Anna; mounted in an enamelled gold setting of the latter end of the sixteenth century, and forming a pretty ornament.

226. Double cameo; oriental onyx of three strata. Height 10 lines; width 8 lines. A very fine stone.

On one side the head of Otho, to the right; on the other, in the white stratum, Vespasian, also to the right.

Good work of the end of the sixteenth or early seventeenth century, in enamelled mounting.

231. Intaglio on oriental agate. Height 1¼ inch; width 1 inch. Head of Massinissa (?), to the left, wearing a helmet, which is ornamented with a *biga* and a hound. Behind the head is a figure of Venus. A copy from the Barberini gem, of Carthaginian Greek work, known as Massinissa, but which Mr. King suggests may represent Hamilcar Barcas.

Fine work, of the latter end of the sixteenth or earlier years of the seventeenth century, after the antique. It is mounted in a silver setting of the eighteenth century, enriched with emeralds, pearls, and rose diamonds.

288. Cameo; white and grey agate. A crowned male head to the right, probably a portrait, in a pretty enamelled gold setting of the same period as the cameo, viz., the sixteenth or seventeenth century.

199. Cameo; fine oriental onyx, brown and white. Height 13 lines; width 10½ lines. An Imperial bust in armour, to the left.

Good work of the later sixteenth or earlier seventeenth century.

56. Cameo; opaque white and clear grey agate. Height 10½ lines; width 13 lines. The triumph of Ariadne.

Fine work of the end of the sixteenth or earlier years of the seventeenth century, in a neat gold setting of the eighteenth.

169. Cameo, on white and grey agate; oval. Height 13 lines; width 11 lines. Head of Antoninus Pius, to the left.

Early and fine work of the seventeenth century.

222. Cameo, on a long oval white and grey agate. Height 10½ lines; width 13 lines. Set in a ring. Neptune in a car drawn by sea-horses. (Plate II.)

Admirable highly-finished work of the seventeenth century, in the spirit and after the manner of Bernini.

235. Cameo; white and grey agate. Height half an inch; width 7½ lines. Set in a ring. Jupiter on an eagle.

In the manner of, and perhaps by the same hand as, No. 222, after the school of Bernini, and of the seventeenth century. I cannot agree with Mr. King, who considers this to be an antique work.

96. Cameo; opaque white and clear agate. Head of a man crying or gaping; of irregular form, about 1 inch in average diameter.

A highly-finished work, probably of the earlier half of the seventeenth century.

This is one of Consul Smith's series, and figured in the *Dactyliotheca*, plate xiii., where it is stated to represent a Typhon, and similar to one on heliotrope in the Medici Cabinet.

148. Cameo, on a white and clear grey agate. Height 1 inch 2 lines; width 11½ lines. Venus, Adonis, and Cupid.

A fine work of the seventeenth century in very high relief.

155. Cameo; agate; white stratum on black. Height 7½ lines; width 6 lines. Female head, to the right. Set as a pendant.

Pretty work of the seventeenth century. From Consul Smith's Collection, figured on plate xix. It is described by him as a " Baccha "

26. A badge or order of the Knights of Malta (?), or more probably of Mount Carmel or St. Lazarus, formed of a plate of gold shaped and enamelled. Diameter 2¾ inches. On the convex face is the Maltese cross in white enamel on a blue ground, with a border of flowers. On the reverse, which is concave, is a central sunk medallion of the Holy Family, surrounded by a border of flowers, in scale-shaped sunken panels edged with gold.

The painting is carefully executed, and may, perhaps, be Spanish work of the seventeenth century.

Two similar badges in the South Kensington Museum have for subject, on one St. John the Baptist preaching in the wilderness ; on the other, the Holy Family with Joseph and the infant St. John. They are by the same hand.

Another, belonging to the Countess Somers, has St. Peter and other saints.

And again another was in the possession of Signor Castellani, with the subject of St. Francis, with views of buildings, &c., at the back.

134. Pendent ornament of enamelled gold, enriched with diamonds, pearls, and rubies, and formed as a pelican " in her piety " in front of a cross set with diamonds. It is suspended by two chains from a jewelled top, to which the ring is attached. Total length about 2¼ inches ; width 1 inch 4 lines. (Plate III.)

Probably Spanish or Portuguese work of the seventeenth century.

98. The Seal of King Charles I. when Prince of Wales, cut on a crystal and set in pale blue enamelled gold, diapered with delicate black ornaments. The quarterings are those of England, France, Scotland, and Ireland, with a label surmounted by the princely crown, with the letters C. R.

141. The Signet Ring of King Charles I. when Prince of Wales.

A large shield-shaped diamond of fine lustre, engraved in intaglio with the Prince of Wales's feathers between the letters C. P., and issuing from a coronet ;

d

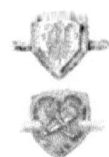

beneath is a ribbon which bears the motto ICH . DIEN. It is set as a ring in enamelled gold, painted behind the bezel with a bow and quiver crossed saltirewise on the dark blue ground. The hoop has a simple edging.   (See woodcut)

This is an extremely elegant and remarkable ring. The engraving on the diamond is executed with great precision, and is deeply cut.

Following the accepted opinion, which was confirmed by Mr. King, I had assumed that this ring was the signet of Charles the Second when Prince of Wales. A little reflection and comparison of dates might, however, have raised some doubt, for when we recollect that the Prince was only nineteen at the date of his father's execution, and the troubled times and impoverished circumstances of the King for years before, it would hardly seem probable that so costly a gem would have been cut for the young Prince's use. That it was the signet used by Charles I. when Prince of Wales is proved by the fact that it seals an autograph letter of his in the possession of the late Mr. Labouchere of Paris. A cast from this was given by Dr. Kendrick of Warrington to the late Mr. Albert Way, and is now in the possession of Mr. Franks.

The art of engraving on the diamond has been ascribed to more than one of the *Renaissance* sculptors. Jacopo da Trezzo, or "Trezzia," being, according to Gorlæus, the discoverer. Clemente Birago, of Milan, is another claimant ; he engraved a portrait of Don Carlos, and the Spanish arms on a diamond, as a seal. The former is said to have cut the arms of Philip II. on the same hard material. In England, about 1557, Jacobus Thronus is said by Gori to have engraved

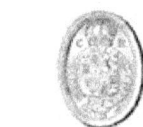

Queen Mary's arms. I should have, however, little hesitation in ascribing Prince Charles's ring to Francis Walwyn, who, in 1628 or 1629, engraved a diamond for King Charles I.[*]

132. The Signet Ring of King Charles I.

A richly ornamented gold hoop, on the shoulders of which are a lion and unicorn of carved steel chiselled in high relief. The bezel is faced with steel and engraved with the Royal arms; quartering, first and fourth, France and England ; second, Scotland; third, Ireland : encircled by the garter, and surmounted by the crown between the letters C. R.

On the gold sides of the bezel the motto DIEU . ET . MON . DROIT . is inserted in letters of steel.   (See woodcuts).

An exquisite piece of metal-work, and of admirable

Vide Walpole's *Anecdotes of Painting* (edited by Wornum, 1849), vol. i. p. 286, note.

design, of the history of which we know nothing. Mr. King inclines to recognise in the engraving the manner of the celebrated Simon, afterwards medallist to the Protector; or, he thinks, it may have been the work of Vanderdoort, who was commanded, on 2nd April, 1625, to make patterns for His Majesty's coins. ("Gems and Rings," p. 406.)

138. An Indian Seal, the handle formed of calcedony, mounted in gold and set with rubies. The seal is an intaglio on glass, and represents a monster, with the sun, moon, &c. Said to have belonged to Tippoo Sahib.

229. Cameo; grey and opaque white agate. Height 11 lines; width 9 lines. Set in a gold ring. A portrait, which may possibly be that of Louis XIV., looking to the right of the spectator, in a raised border. Signed NATTER. (Plate II.)

The hair, long behind, is dressed in a peak over the forehead. Mr. King refers to this cameo as probably a portrait of William III.

71. Intaglio on a large oval cornelian. Height 2 inches 2 lines; width 1 inch 8 lines. St. George and the Dragon, to the left. Signed BERINI. F.

Mounted in gold with the garter and motto.

223. Cameo; cornelian Height 1 inch; width ⅞-inch. A male *portrait* head to the right, with long hair.

A fine and probably English work of the early part of the eighteenth century

140. Intaglio on a fine brown sard. Set in a ring. Ariadne, from the antique statue in the Vatican.

A very fine work. Signed MARCHANT. F. ROMA.

181. Intaglio on a choice oriental onyx, cut through the brown to the white layer. Height 1½ inch; width 1 inch ¼ line. Head of Bacchus. Set in a ring. Signed BURCH. R.A.

A remarkably fine work.

102. Intaglio on cornelian. Height 9½ lines. Head of Antinous (?), to the left. Signed PICLER. Set in a gold ring.

118. Cameo; oval; red and white agate. A lion *couchant*. Signed BURCH. Set in a gold ring.

130. Cameo; oval; onyx of two strata. Height 1 inch 1½ line; width 1 inch. Three-quarter bust portrait of a lady, to the right, in a costume of the time of Louis XV. (Plate III.)

In an elegant mounting of silver, as a medallion, set with diamonds and rubies; workmanship of the eighteenth century. Probably the portrait of Clementina

Sobieski wife of the first Pretender. It has, however, been suggested that this cameo may be a portrait of one of the daughters of George II.

200. Intaglio on cornelian. Height 10½ lines; width 8¼ lines. Set in a gold ring.

Portrait of King George III. when a young man; a work of that period.

202. Intaglio on cornelian. Height 6½ lines; width 6 lines. Set in a gold ring.

Portrait of King George III. in middle age; a work of that period, of able execution, and signed KIRK. 1.

.

www.ingramcontent.com/pod-product-compliance
Lightning Source LLC
Chambersburg PA
CBHW021450090426
42739CB00009B/1706